American Moments

ABDO
Daughters

THE PONY EXPRESS

By Alan Pierce

Published by ABDO Publishing Company, 4940 Viking Drive, Suite 622, Edina, Minnesota 55435. Copyright © 2005 by Abdo Consulting Group, Inc. International copyrights reserved in all countries. No part of this book may be reproduced in any form without written permission from the publisher. ABDO & Daughters™ is a trademark and logo of ABDO Publishing Company.

Printed in the United States.

Edited by: Melanie A. Howard
Interior Production and Design: Terry Dunham Incorporated
Cover Design: Mighty Media
Photos: Corbis, Library of Congress

Library of Congress Cataloging-in-Publication Data

Pierce, Alan, 1966-
    The Pony Express / Alan Pierce.
        p. cm. -- (American moments)
    Includes index.
    ISBN 1-59197-938-2
    1. Pony express--History--Juvenile literature. 2. Postal service--United States--History--Juvenile literature. I. Title. II. Series.

HE6375.P65P54 2005
383'.18--dc22
                                                                    2004062724

CONTENTS

UNKOWN RIDER, FAMOUS RIDE

In the darkness of evening, a rider on horseback galloped out of St. Joseph, Missouri. Nobody knows the name of the rider who raced off on April 3, 1860. Some believe it was Johnny Frey or Frye. Others think Billy Richardson rode the horse. A few claim another man was the rider. In any case, this person was the first rider of the Pony Express.

The Pony Express delivered the mail. It relied on a relay of horses and riders to carry mail between St. Joseph and Sacramento, California. This 1,966-mile (3,164-km) route crossed deserts, the Rocky Mountains, and the Sierra Nevada. California and the future states of Kansas, Nebraska, Colorado, Wyoming, Utah, and Nevada were part of this trail. The route was dotted with stations about 12 miles (19 km) apart where riders switched horses.

Advertisements had declared that the Pony Express would deliver mail to California in nine days or less. This was much faster than the current rate of delivery. Most mail from the eastern United States took three weeks or more to arrive in California. Californians wanted a faster mail service. The Pony Express promised to fill that need.

On April 13, the mail carried by the first Pony Express rider reached Sacramento. People in the city were thrilled to get news that

People in Sacramento celebrate the arrival of the first Pony Express rider.

was only 10 days old. They cheered and filled the sidewalks to see the first rider from the east. Californians also rang bells and fired cannons to celebrate.

Despite this enthusiasm, the Pony Express did not last long. It existed 18 months, and lost thousands of dollars for its owners. The Pony Express was an ambitious idea, but it faced many challenges in the mid-nineteenth century.

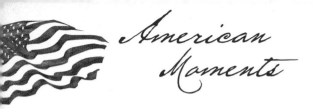
THE TELEGRAPH

One challenge to the Pony Express was the telegraph. This invention used electricity and wires to deliver messages almost immediately. In the early 1800s, scientists had made discoveries that made the telegraph possible. Alessandro Volta had made a type of electric battery in present-day Italy. Later, the Danish scientist Hans Christian Ørsted experimented with electric currents and magnetic needles.

In the United States, Samuel F.B. Morse was primarily responsible for the telegraph. Morse was born in Charlestown, Massachusetts, on April 27, 1791. As a young man, he studied at Yale College, which is now Yale University, in New Haven, Connecticut. In college, Morse attended lectures about electricity. However, he was far more interested in painting, and he wished to become an artist. In 1811, Morse left the United States to study art in England.

Morse returned to the United States in 1815. He made a living by painting portraits. Morse was an excellent artist, but it was hard to get work. During this time, Morse married Lucretia Walker in 1818. Seven years later, she died after the birth of one of their children. Morse's parents died within the next few years. In 1829, he sailed to Europe to deal with his grief.

Morse left Europe in 1832. While aboard the ship *Sully* he met Charles Thomas Jackson, who had studied medicine. The two men

Samuel F.B. Morse tests the telegraph.

talked about recent developments in electricity. These discussions gave Morse an idea. While sailing back to the United States, he began drawing plans for a telegraph.

During the next few years, Morse dedicated most of his efforts toward his painting. However, by 1837, he had made a device that could transmit messages over 1,700 feet (518 m) of wire. That same year, he applied for a patent for his invention. The next year, Morse developed a code for sending messages. This system became known as Morse Code. It uses dashes, dots, and spaces to represent letters and punctuation.

Morse asked Congress for funds to set up a telegraph. Finally, in 1843, Congress approved $30,000 to build a telegraph line between Washington DC and Baltimore, Maryland. On May 24, 1844, Morse was ready to test his telegraph. In Washington DC, he transmitted the Biblical passage "What hath God wrought!"

Morse's demonstration did not mean quick success for the telegraph. Other scientists believed they should get credit for the telegraph. Morse and these scientists soon became involved in lawsuits. These legal problems hindered the telegraph for a few years.

Samuel F.B. Morse

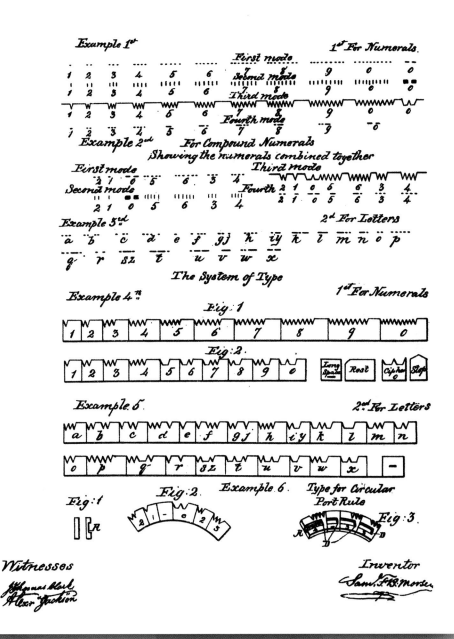

Morse Code chart

WAR AND GOLD

The telegraph was experiencing some difficulties. Nevertheless, it accustomed some Americans to faster communication. Meanwhile, communication and travel continued to improve because of the railroad. In the 1840s, the miles of railroad track grew in the United States. Before trains, a journey from New York City, New York, to St. Louis, Missouri, took three weeks. Trains later cut this trip to three days.

While travel and communications improved, the size of the United States expanded. In the 1840s, U.S. president James K. Polk was interested in buying California from Mexico. But the Mexican government was unhappy with the United States. The United States had already annexed Texas, which had formerly been part of Mexico. Mexicans were not interested in selling California to the United States.

The border between Mexico and Texas was unclear at this time. In January 1846, Polk ordered General Zachary Taylor to lead troops into a disputed area. This land was between the Nueces River and the Rio Grande. It was a dangerous act since the Mexican government believed the Nueces River marked the border between the two nations. On April 25, Mexican soldiers attacked Taylor's troops. The U.S. Congress declared war on Mexico on May 13.

The U.S. military won several victories against the Mexican army. General Stephen Kearny invaded present-day New Mexico and then

The discovery of gold at Sutter's Mill resulted in the California gold rush.

marched his army into California. Meanwhile, U.S. Army captain
John C. Frémont helped overthrow Mexican rule in California.
General Taylor also defeated Mexican forces in the northern part of the
country. The decisive victory came when U.S. general Winfield Scott
captured the Mexican capital, Mexico City, on September 14, 1847.

On January 24, 1848, California became more valuable to the
United States. About 40 miles (64 km) from Sacramento, a carpenter
named James W. Marshall discovered yellow particles in a branch of
the American River. These particles turned out to be gold. Marshall
was building a mill for a Swiss immigrant named John A. Sutter.
Sutter wanted the discovery to be kept secret until he could obtain
legal protection for his property.

A few days after this discovery, California officially became part of the United States. On February 2, 1848, representatives from the two nations signed the Treaty of Guadalupe Hidalgo. The treaty ended the Mexican War and ceded a vast amount of Mexican territory to the United States. The United States gained 500,000 square miles (1.3 million sq km) of land from Mexico. This was nearly half of Mexico's territory. In addition to California, this territory made up all or part of the future states of New Mexico, Utah, Nevada, Arizona, and Colorado.

A month after the treaty, news about the gold discovery spread in California. People from the California cities of San Francisco and Monterey headed to the Sierra Nevada to mine gold. By summer, Americans in the eastern United States had heard about the gold discovery. Americans hoping to get rich began pouring into California. The California gold rush had begun.

Americans in the eastern part of the country used different routes to reach California. But the journey to California was difficult. The Panama Canal did not exist yet to shorten the voyage between the coasts. No railroads crossed the country. Instead, some gold seekers sailed around Cape Horn at the southern tip of South America. This voyage took about six months. Others took ships to the Isthmus of Panama. They crossed the narrow strip of land and continued by ship to the west coast.

Both of these voyages were dangerous. The South Atlantic Ocean was often stormy and caused rough conditions at sea around Cape Horn. The shorter trip through the isthmus was also risky. Deadly diseases such as cholera, malaria, and yellow fever thrived on the isthmus.

A man uses a cradle to mine for gold in a river in California. A cradle is a rocking device used for panning gold.

Most Americans chose to reach California by land. Overland routes were shorter than traveling by sea. The journey from the Missouri River to California was about 2,000 miles (3,219 km). Many fortune hunters traveled in groups of covered wagons pulled by horses, mules, or oxen. The overland trails, however, were also dangerous. Diseases such as cholera and dysentery killed many travelers.

President Polk stressed the importance of communication with Americans in the West. This goal was critical as settlers headed to California and the Oregon Territory. Also, thousands of Mormons had settled near the Great Salt Lake in the 1840s. They had moved west to flee the persecution they had faced in the eastern United States.

To organize mail service, the federal government set up a post office in San Francisco, California, in 1848. A year later, a post office was established in Salt Lake City in the Utah Territory.

Thousands of people arrived in California in 1849. They became known as forty-niners. But Americans were not the only treasure seekers. People from China,

James K. Polk

Cartoon showing lawlessness in California

Ireland, and from what is now Germany streamed to the goldfields. These migrations increased California's population dramatically. Before the gold rush, about 14,000 non-Native Americans lived in California. By the end of 1849, the number of people had climbed to about 100,000.

Lawlessness and violence became serious problems as California's population grew. Bandits attacked ranches. Murder and robbery became common at mining camps. Groups of vigilantes tried to impose justice. But these groups often committed violence.

Californians took steps to establish order in the territory. They formed a government as if California were a state. On October 10, 1849, Californians approved a constitution, and soon chose a governor and legislators. Congress accepted California's admission into the Union on September 9, 1850.

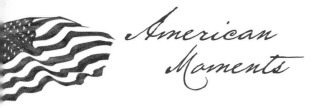

A CRAVING FOR MAIL

California was filled with people who wanted news from their families in the eastern United States. Miners in the goldfields were known to pay a great deal of money for mail. Some paid as much as an ounce (28.3 g) of gold dust for a letter. Today, that would be like paying $300 for a piece of mail.

In San Francisco, people waited anxiously for ships carrying the mail. Those expecting mail often waited for days in line at the post office. Miners even offered gold dust to buy a place in line.

At this time, ships transported the mail to California. They followed the same route as many of the gold seekers. Ships from the East Coast sailed to the Isthmus of Panama. From there, the mail was transported overland to another ship that sailed to California.

In 1855, a railroad was constructed across the isthmus. This made mail delivery somewhat faster. Mail could now travel from the East Coast to California in about three weeks. However, this route was not always dependable. Bad weather sometimes delayed ships and even sank them.

An attempt was made to use an overland route to deliver mail in the western United States. George Chorpenning and Absalom Woodward received a federal contract to deliver mail in 1851. The contract called for hauling mail between Sacramento and Salt Lake City. Another man, Samuel H. Woodson, completed the

Californians swarm the post office to get mail.

overland route. He received a contract to deliver mail between Salt Lake City and Independence, Missouri.

Chorpenning and Woodward encountered many obstacles that made mail delivery in the West so risky. Their 750-mile (1,207-km) route crossed the towering Sierra Nevada in eastern California. This mountain range has peaks as high as 14,000 feet (4,270 m) above sea level. Heavy snowfall in the mountains delayed service.

The contract called for delivering the mail in 30 days. Instead, it took more than 50 days. Also, Shoshone Native Americans killed Woodward. Nevertheless, Chorpenning continued to deliver mail throughout the 1850s.

This attempt showed how difficult it was to deliver mail under such severe conditions. The distances were long and crossed deserts and mountains. In addition, tribes of hostile Native Americans lived in some of these areas.

Meanwhile, other ways were being looked at to link the east and west coasts. One option was the telegraph. By 1850, thousands of miles of telegraph wire had been

18

Jefferson Davis

The Sierra Nevada

built in the United States. But no telegraph line existed between California and the rest of the nation. Constructing a transcontinental telegraph would be difficult. Cable would have to be strung over mountains and deserts. Also, the line would pass through Native American land. The telegraph would depend on their acceptance for success.

The railroad offered another way to connect the east and west coasts. In 1853, Congress passed the Pacific Railroad Survey Bill. This legislation authorized U.S. secretary of war Jefferson Davis to proceed with explorations of the West. The purpose of the expeditions was to find routes for a railroad. Eventually, teams of soldiers found possible routes. But leaders in government disagreed about which route to choose.

The telegraph and railroad were making progress. But in the 1850s, they were not able to cross the vast distance between the coasts. And people in the West were not satisfied with the speed of communication. In 1856, about 75,000 Californians signed a petition calling for better mail service.

The next year, the U.S. Postal Service accepted bids for another mail and passenger service. This service would run between the Mississippi River and San Francisco. U.S. postmaster general Aaron V. Brown accepted a proposal from John Butterfield.

Butterfield favored a 2,800-mile (4,506-km) southern route between Tipton, Missouri, and San Francisco. This route went through Arkansas to El Paso, Texas, and then west to Los Angeles, California. The route then went northward through the California Valley. Many people criticized this route. It was considerably longer

A Butterfield Overland Mail Company stagecoach

than other proposed routes. However, Brown argued that the weather was better along the southern path.

In 1858, the Butterfield Overland Mail Company began its stagecoach service along the southern route. The company began with 500 stagecoaches, 1,000 horses, and about 800 men. Stations were set up along the route where fresh teams of horses were kept. These stations existed about every 8 to 25 miles (13 to 40 km) along the route. The company's stagecoaches could travel from Missouri to San Francisco in about 24 days.

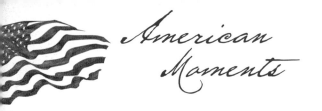

THE PONY EXPRESS

The Butterfield Overland Mail Company was not the only business that had established a supply line in the West. The firm of Russell, Majors, and Waddell used wagons pulled by oxen to deliver supplies to U.S. army forts. This company was formed by William R. Russell, Alexander Majors, and William B. Waddell.

Each business partner carried out a different task. Waddell handled the company's finances. Majors was in charge of day-to-day operations. But Majors was also a religious man who demanded that his employees act decently. He required workers to take an oath. In the oath, employees promised "not to use profane language, not to get drunk, not to gamble, nor to treat the animals cruelly . . . "

Russell promoted the company in the eastern United States. He worked with politicians and bankers to get money and government contracts. Many people believe the plan for the Pony Express emerged from one of Russell's meetings in 1859. In Washington DC, U.S. senator William Gwin of California proposed an idea to Russell. Gwin was interested in another mail route to compete with Butterfield's southern mail route.

As part of this idea, Gwin wanted to conduct an experiment. He wished to see whether reliable mail service could be established over the Rocky Mountains and Sierra Nevada. Russell shared the senator's

William Gwin

idea with Majors and Waddell. There was a tempting reason for trying the mail service. Russell claimed Gwin would help the company get a government contract to deliver the mail. But first, Russell, Majors, and Waddell had to prove the company could carry mail across the West.

On January 27, 1860, Russell, Majors, and Waddell established a company to carry out this experiment. The company was called Central Overland California and Pikes Peak Express Company. It was better known as the Pony Express.

The three men had two months to set up the route, build stations, hire riders, and acquire horses. Fortunately, choosing the route was not difficult. Russell had run stagecoaches between St. Joseph and Salt Lake City. The company, however, had to establish a new route between Salt Lake City and Sacramento.

Workers fanned out from Denver in present-day Colorado, Salt Lake City, and Sacramento to build stations. These stations were furnished with stoves, axes, hammers, and other equipment.

This is the Pony Express station in St. Joseph, Missouri. It is now a Pony Express museum.

In order to cover this long route, Majors believed the company would need 400 to 500 horses. The company purchased horses throughout the west. These horses were then taken to the stations.

The Pony Express also needed riders who could endure hardships. However, tough did not mean big. The company wanted riders built like jockeys. Most Pony Express riders weighed between 100 and 120 pounds (45 to 54 kg). Historians disagree about the ages of Pony Express riders. Some historians believe the riders were mostly young men between the ages of 18 and 20. Others believe the riders came from a wider age group.

In addition to toughness in its riders, the Pony Express wanted upstanding employees. Bibles bound in calfskin were given to the riders. Also, each rider had to sign Major's oath when hired.

Bibles and mail weren't the only items the riders carried. Each rider was armed with a rifle and two Colt revolvers. However, Pony Express riders were not encouraged to fight. They were told to try to outrun any trouble they might encounter.

The Pony Express tended to hire local men as riders. Many riders for the eastern portion of the route came from the Kansas and Nebraska territories and Missouri. Around Salt Lake City, Mormon riders carried the mail. However, immigrants from France and modern-day Germany also served as riders.

In March 1860, advertisements appeared that announced the arrival of the Pony Express. These advertisements promised mail delivery in eight or nine days from the East Coast to San Francisco. Russell, Majors, and Waddell then got the Pony Express running. On April 3, 1860, the first Pony Express rider bolted from St. Joseph. The mail was rushing to California as advertised.

The Simpson Springs Pony Express station provided supplies for riders in the Utah Territory. The stone building is a replica of one of the buildings that stood at the site. Simpson Springs was one of more than 100 outposts that the Pony Express operated. The Pony Express managed two kinds of stations. The larger stations were known as "home" stations, while smaller stations were called "relay rider" stations. Home stations were located about 65 to 100 miles (105 to 161 km) apart. Relay rider stations were separated by 12 to 15 miles (19 to 24 km). At home stations, a station keeper oversaw five or six employees. Each relay rider station was usually attended by one or two employees who took care of the horses.

PONY BOB'S DARING RIDE

The Pony Express started with 80 riders. Each mail carrier rode about 75 miles (121 km). He switched horses at stations along the way to maintain fresh mounts. The riders carried the mail in a pouch called a mochila. *Mochila* is a Spanish word for knapsack. The mochila was made of leather and had four pockets. The mochila was easy for the riders to use. They could quickly slip it over their saddles when they changed horses.

The mail carried by the Pony Express was printed on a special lightweight paper. This paper was wrapped in oiled silk for protection. The mail was not supposed to weigh more than 10 pounds (4.5 kg).

For many riders, weather and the difficulty of long rides in the saddle were their greatest enemies. Riders braved blizzards and rainstorms. Sometimes they ran the risk of losing the trail in the snow.

A few weeks into the operation, the Pony Express experienced a crisis. In present-day Nevada, relations between whites and Native Americans had been bad for decades. This situation worsened when silver was discovered in the Washoe Hills in 1859. Whites flooded into the area and took over land and water claimed by the Paiute Native Americans. The Pony Express had also set up stations at important water sources.

On May 7, 1860, Native Americans burned down a small settlement known as Williams Station. Five to seven people were killed in the attack. It is unknown whether the station was part of the Pony Express. In any case, the attack alarmed whites in the region.

Two days later, Pony Express rider Robert "Pony Bob" Haslam set off from Friday's Station. The station was located near present-day Lake Tahoe, Nevada. He rode east to Carson City where there were no relief horses. He pushed on to Buckland's Station. Haslam had completed his 75-mile (121-km) part of the route.

A mochila

At Buckland's Station, the relief rider refused to go on. No rider had been known to shirk his duty. The station keeper reportedly offered Haslam $50 to continue riding. Haslam agreed, and proceeded to ride across the desert until he reached Smith's Creek Station. Here, Haslam finally slept. He had ridden 190 miles (306 km) without rest.

Haslam was not through riding. After sleeping about eight hours, Haslam rode back west with a mochila. He discovered a grim sight at the Cold Springs Station. The Paiutes had destroyed the station and killed the station keeper.

Haslam continued on to the Sand Springs Station where he warned the station keeper about the danger. The keeper and Haslam fled the station. Haslam rode west until he reached Buckland's Station again. In 36 hours, he had ridden 380 miles (612 km) in the midst of hostilities. Haslam's feat is considered one of the most famous rides of the Pony Express.

The conflict with the Paiutes was known as the Pyramid Lake War. It took an awful toll on the Pony Express. Native Americans attacked stations along a 300-mile (483-km) stretch of the route. As many as 17 Pony Express employees were killed.

The violence forced the Pony Express to quit deliveries between Carson City and Salt Lake City. Accounts disagree on how long the service was shut down, but the loss of service cost the company $75,000. U.S. troops and volunteers fought the Paiutes in May, but Native Americans continued to attack Pony Express stations.

Not all the violence on the Pony Express trail occurred between Native Americans and whites. On July 12, 1861, a shooting occurred at the Rock Creek Station in the Nebraska Territory. Pony Express

Settlers meet with Native Americans near Pyramid Lake in the Utah Territory. Pyramid Lake takes its name from the pyramid-like rock formation seen in this picture.

employees killed David McCanles and two other men. One of the employees involved in the shooting was James Butler Hickok. He was not a rider for the Pony Express, but he tended livestock at the station.

There are different accounts of the shooting. Some describe McCanles as an outlaw. Others claim McCanles arrived unarmed at the station to collect money. Whatever the truth, the shooting helped launch the legend of "Wild Bill" Hickok. Hickok went on to become a celebrated lawman in Kansas.

Another popular story is that William F. Cody was a rider for the Pony Express. Cody later became better known as the legendary frontiersman "Buffalo Bill." Cody claimed to have been a Pony Express rider. Majors, who became Cody's friend, wrote that Cody rode for the Pony Express.

Many historians agree that Cody delivered messages for Russell, Majors, and Waddell in 1857. Cody would have been 11 years old at the time. However, some have concluded that Cody probably never rode for the Pony Express.

James Butler Hickok

32

William F. Cody

THE BEGINNING OF A LEGEND

The Pony Express faced difficulties caused by bad weather and Native American conflicts. But another threat created an even bigger problem for the Pony Express. The company lost money. It is estimated that the company lost $30 for every letter the Pony Express delivered. Some employees joked about the business's name Central Overland California and Pikes Peak Express Company. They said COCPP really stood for "Clean Out of Cash and Poor Pay."

Meanwhile, some people considered a transcontinental telegraph. Congress helped this undertaking by approving the Pacific Telegraph Act in June 1860. This law set aside $40,000 a year for any company that would install a telegraph line between Missouri and San Francisco. The Western Union and Missouri Telegraph Company received the contract for this project.

Russell also wanted a federal contract to help the Pony Express. He campaigned for a federal contract in Washington DC. Such a contract would bring in money. But, Russell did not have much luck until a national disaster actually benefited his company.

This crisis occurred during the winter of 1860–1861, when several Southern states left the nation. On February 1, 1861, Texas seceded from the United States. These states formed the Confederate States of America. Southern troops stopped the mail route that went through

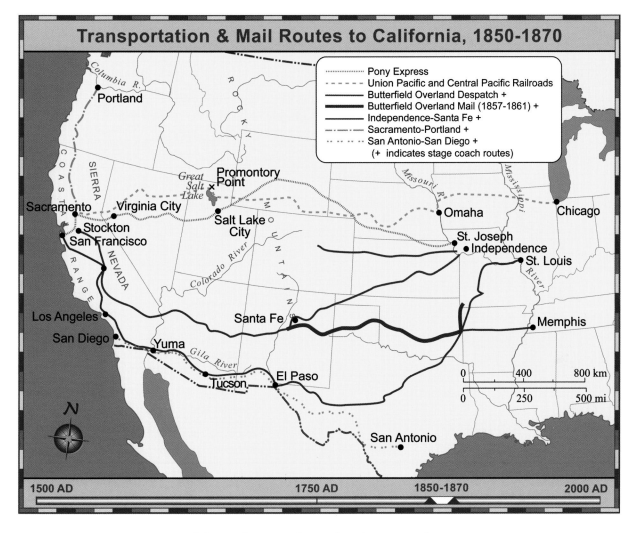

Map of several overland routes that delivered mail and supplies to California

southern Missouri and Texas. Congress did not want to depend on a southern mail route. It decided to support the more northern mail route to California.

In March 1861, Congress approved a contract. The contract provided the Pony Express with $470,000 to operate the eastern part of the mail route. However, the government's support was limited. It would only last until a telegraph line had been built between California and the rest of the country.

The Pony Express was a financial failure. But it did accomplish its purpose of speeding up mail delivery service across the country. Most of the time, the Pony Express was dependable. In the spring and summer, mail delivery averaged about 12 days. In the fall and winter, delivery usually took about 14 days.

The fastest Pony Express ride took place in March 1861. Riders hurried President Abraham Lincoln's Inaugural Address to California in 7 days and 17 hours. In the speech, Lincoln discussed the prospect of civil war. The decision of the Southern states to leave the nation had caused the crisis. In his speech, Lincoln still offered hope for a peaceful solution.

The crisis had highlighted the importance of the Pony Express. Newspapers carried by the Pony Express kept Westerners informed about troubling developments in the East. By April 1861, the Civil War broke out between the Northern and Southern states. Californians relied on the Pony Express to learn about events in the war.

But even at its fastest, the Pony Express could not compete with the telegraph. Construction of the transcontinental telegraph took less time than expected. For the most part, the line followed the route of the Pony Express. Still, building the line was an amazing feat. Some equipment had to be shipped from New York City to California. Work in the desert was also challenging. Water had to be brought in for the crews.

In October 1861, the overland telegraph was completed. California was connected by wire with the eastern half of the country. In addition to being faster, the telegraph was also cheaper. Businesses paid as much as $150 to send mail by Pony Express. A message by telegraph cost about $50. The Pony Express ended in October 1861. After 18 months of operation, it had lost an estimated $400,000.

A Pony Express rider races to deliver mail.

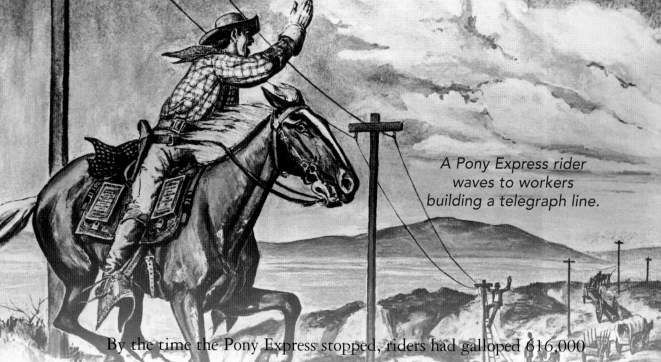

A Pony Express rider waves to workers building a telegraph line.

By the time the Pony Express stopped, riders had galloped 616,000 miles (991,356 km) and transported 35,000 pieces of mail. During its months of operation, the Pony Express had provided a valuable service for Californians. The Pony Express sped communication between California and the rest of the nation. Faster communication gave some businesses an advantage over others that did not use the Pony Express.

Although the Pony Express had a brief existence, people did not forget it. William F. Cody kept the memory of the Pony Express alive. Cody served with the Union army during the Civil War. Later, he was a scout during wars with Native Americans. His exploits as a buffalo hunter earned him the nickname "Buffalo Bill." Sensational stories about Cody appeared in dime novels.

In 1883, Cody used his fame to establish Buffalo Bill's Wild West show. Cody starred in this show, which included expert riders and sharpshooters. He also included a demonstration of the Pony Express in the performance. People from all over the United States saw Cody's show. Buffalo Bill's Wild West show also toured Europe. Queen Victoria of Britain enjoyed this American form of entertainment.

The Pony Express continued to be celebrated in books, paintings, and movies. One of the first movies about the Pony Express was made in 1907. Many others followed. Later images and words helped create the memory of the Pony Express. But Americans tend not to remember the failed enterprise that lasted 18 months. Instead, they think of the swift horses and hardy riders who dashed across the West. The legend of the Pony Express continues to gallop on in the hearts and imaginations of the American people.

Cody and a Native American perform a scene in Buffalo Bill's Wild West show.

A poster advertises Buffalo Bill's Wild West show. Posters such as this appeared in stores and on buildings. They were one of the most effective ways of advertising the Wild West show. Buffalo Bill's Wild West show was extremely popular. People lined up to buy tickets, even though admission was expensive for most families.

Audiences could expect to see acts that featured expert horsemanship and marksmanship. Although some acts changed over the years, demonstrations of the Pony Express always remained part of the show. A former Pony Express rider named Billy Johnson showed how riders quickly changed horses. This performance helped preserve the memory of the Pony Express.

ILL'S WILD WEST
ROUGH RIDERS OF THE WORLD.

COPYRIGHT 1899

Courier
LITHO. CO.
BUFFALO
N.Y.

COL. W. F. CODY
"BUFFALO BILL"
WILL APPEAR
AT EVERY PERFORMANCE

OYS, THE REAL ROUGH RIDERS OF THE WORLD WHOSE DARING EXPLOITS
HAVE MADE THEIR VERY NAMES SYNONYMOUS WITH DEEDS OF BRAVERY.

TIMELINE

1846 to 1848 The Mexican War is fought between the United States and Mexico.

1848 On January 24, gold is discovered in California.

The U.S. government sets up a post office in San Francisco, California.

1851 George Chorpenning, Absalom Woodward, and Samuel H. Woodson receive contracts to deliver mail between Sacramento, California, and Independence, Missouri.

1856 About 75,000 Californians sign a petition asking for better mail service.

1858 The Butterfield Overland Mail Company begins a stagecoach service to shuttle mail and people between Tipton, Missouri, and San Francisco.

1859 William R. Russell, Alexander Majors, and William B. Waddell accept the challenge of creating an overland mail route over the Rocky Mountains and Sierra Nevada.

1860 On January 27, Russell, Majors, and Waddell establish the Central Overland California and Pikes Peak Express Company or Pony Express.

On April 3, the Pony Express begins with the first ride to deliver mail between St. Joseph, Missouri, and Sacramento.

On April 13, the mail from the first ride reaches Sacramento.

Native Americans burn down Williams Station on May 7. This sparks the Pyramid Lake War.

On May 9, Robert "Pony Bob" Haslam begins the 380-mile (612-km) ride that helped make the Pony Express famous. The ride takes Haslam 36 hours.

1861

Congress approves a contract giving $470,000 in funding to the Pony Express. This funding is slated to last only until the transcontinental telegraph line is completed.

The fastest ride of the pony express takes place in March. Riders carrying President Abraham Lincoln's Inaugural Address deliver the address to California in 7 days and 17 hours.

By April, the Civil War begins.

In October, the transcontinental telegraph is completed. The Pony Express ends.

American Moments

FAST FACTS

When the Civil War began, Pony Express riders were required to swear an oath of allegiance to the Union along with Alexander Majors's oath.

American author Samuel Langhorne Clemens, better known as Mark Twain, was fascinated by the Pony Express. Thirty-five years before an official account was given, Twain described the enterprise. He included a description of Pony Express riders and their route in his book *Roughing It* in 1872. *Roughing It* is an autobiography about Clemens's many adventures in the West.

Buffalo Bill Cody's Wild West show featured several famous people. These included the sharpshooter Annie Oakley, Buck Taylor, Johnny Baker, Pawnee Bill, and Chief Sitting Bull. Shows such as this helped build the image of the "wild west."

The Pony Express route is currently a National Historic Trail maintained by the National Park Service. There are approximately 120 historic sites along the trail, though not all of them are yet available to the public. Fifty of these sites are former Pony Express stations.

One of the legends of the Pony Express is an advertisement for riders. Part of the ad asks for "Young, skinny, wiry fellows, not over eighteen. Must be expert riders, willing to risk death daily. Orphans preferred." This ad supposedly appeared in a San Francisco, California, newspaper. However, the source of the ad has never been found.

WEB SITES
WWW.ABDOPUB.COM

Would you like to learn more about the Pony Express? Please visit **www.abdopub.com** to find up-to-date Web site links about the Pony Express and other American moments. These links are routinely monitored and updated to provide the most current information available.

This monument shows the three men who founded the Pony Express.

GLOSSARY

annex: to add land to a nation.

cholera: a disease of the intestines that includes severe vomiting and diarrhea.

Confederate States of America: the country formed by the states of South Carolina, Georgia, Florida, Alabama, Louisiana, Mississippi, Texas, Virginia, Tennessee, Arkansas, and North Carolina that left the Union between 1860 and 1861. It is also called the Confederacy.

dime novel: a paperback book that generally contains many exaggerations.

dysentery: a disease that causes severe diarrhea.

inaugural address: speech given by an official when he or she is sworn into office.

isthmus: a narrow strip of land connecting two larger areas.

lawsuit: a case brought to court because of a perceived wrong.

malaria: a disease spread by mosquitoes that causes chills and fever.

Mormon: a member of the Church of Jesus Christ of Latter-day Saints. This group believes in the Book of Mormon as set forth by Joseph Smith in 1830.

patent: a document granting a right or privilege.

profane: crude or offensive.

transcontinental: crossing a continent.

vigilante: one who takes law enforcement into his or her own hands.

wrought: caused or made, worked.

yellow fever: a tropical disease transmitted by mosquitoes. Symptoms include headache, backache, fever, nausea, and vomiting. If patients do not recover, they can die within six to seven days of experiencing symptoms.

INDEX